ORIGINALLY RED®

Be Bold. Be Brave. Be YOU.

Nicole Michelle Pertillar

R RAIN
PUBLISHING

KNIGHTDALE, NORTH CAROLINA

Nicole Michelle Pertillar/Rain Publishing, LLC
PO Box 702
Knightdale, NC 27545
http://www.rainpublishing.com/

Originally RED/ Nicole Michelle Pertillar. – softcover ed.
ISBN 978-0-9962421-4-1

Kamryn Adams
Amanda Adomatis
Krisette Cole
Felicia Craig
Valerie Hall
Rachel Renee Smith

*Thank you for sharing your hearts for this project.
Your words inspired me and gave shape to what
God wanted to share with His daughters.*

"...but in the moment when one turns toward the Lord, the veil is removed. By "the Lord" what I mean is the Spirit, and in any heart where the Spirit of the Lord is present, there is liberty. Now all of us, with our faces unveiled, reflect the glory of the Lord as if we are mirrors; and so we are being transformed, metamorphosed, into His same image from one radiance of glory to another, just as the Spirit of the Lord accomplishes it."

~2 Corinthians 3:16-18(The Voice)

Originally RED® describes the beginning of my journey to being transformed into HIS image. It's about my unveiling. My prayer is that it inspires you to either start or go deeper into your own journey and teach others to do the same.

CONTENTS

Foreword

Every once in a while a person crosses your path, and you can feel the surge of destiny and purpose emanating through her pores. Nicole Pertillar is such a woman. I could not tell you the date and time that I first met Nicole; however, I still recall the day she shared with me one of her dreams. From that moment, I felt connected to her. Some people's dreams capture our hearts because in some way they are our dreams too.

The first time I walked into Nicole's bedroom I noticed a great big, red dot hanging on her wall. I wondered where the sentence was that preceded that period. It wasn't there, just a big, bright red dot.

Are you ready for this? You can choose to make a statement on this earth, or you can choose to just be a dot among all the other dots in the world. You can make your dot a declaration by adding a sentence before it.

What does your sentence say?
What is your purpose?
Who are you?

Are you anxious to make a statement about yourself, your purpose, and your faith before your red dot? If so, then you are reading the right book. This book is written by a real person. What do I mean by that? If you've ever read the Velveteen Rabbit by Margery Williams then you know that the rabbit became real after he was loved by the boy. However, the love that the rabbit received didn't leave him looking as pristine as when he was new. Nicole has experienced both love and heartache, and she is courageous enough to discuss it. If you're looking for someone to give you an easy fix, this is not the book for you.

Originally RED® will inspire you to become the BEST you! There is greatness inside of you! Your lineage is royalty. You have purpose. Sometimes in order to determine our purpose, we have to shift our focus. Stop staring at the dot, and start making a statement. You are enough. If you can't find the strength to make a whole sentence, then just put one word in front of that dot. Describe yourself for the world. As God motivates you, inspires you, and heals you through Nicole's words, be brave enough to search for the truth.

Remember, you don't have to be anybody else. You were created to be you. You were designed to be one of a kind. Be Bold. Be Brave. Be YOU. Be Originally RED®, and be FREE!

~Kristin Reeg, Author and Freedom Chick, KristinReeg.com

Introduction

I'm 37 years old and I've been a Christian since I was eleven. In spite of walking with the Lord for quite a while, I am just beginning to feel as though I have a handle on who I truly am. I know some aspects of identity can only come with age and experience. However, I firmly believe there are some fundamental truths about who God created us to be that, if learned early on, will enable people to navigate life with much less heartache and drama than many of us faced in childhood and throughout our young adult lives.

I want nothing more than to help young women avoid many of the patterns and beliefs that have tripped me up over the years. Toxic relationships and faulty beliefs kept me bound in hurtful habits and mindsets. I lived a life beneath what I was called to be living. I want to stop this cycle in young women and girls. I believe one of the best ways to do that is to speak to the hearts of their mothers, grandmothers, aunts, teachers and mentors: YOU.

I love little girls. My heart is for them. I desire them to know who they are, understand they are fully loved and be confident in that from a young age. As a former little girl, I know how hard life can be. Far too often and much too soon little girls lose the joy and delight of being girls. Because they don't understand how special they are, they grow up fighting for love, fighting for acceptance, fighting to fit in; fighting to be understood; fighting for protection. They obtain scars from a fight that has already been won for them. They simply don't understand that truth.

Our baby girls don't understand because we, the significant women in their lives, don't understand it about ourselves. Life happens. Wounds happen. Disappointments happen. We are bombarded with media messages dictating to us who we are and how we should act. Our husbands don't meet our lofty expectations (that only God can meet), or we've never been chosen to be a wife. Or maybe your husband left. Maybe you struggle with Daddy issues. Whatever the case may be for you, I want you to know that YOU ARE INDEED AN ORIGINAL MASTERPIECE with value and worth. The fight for your identity has already been won. You are the daughter of a King, which undoubtedly makes you a princess. We need a major SHIFT in our thinking because truthfully, how many of you truly feel like princesses?

By definition, a princess is a female member of a royal family, especially a daughter or granddaughter of a king or queen. When you gave your life to the Lord, you became the daughter of The King. Through that relationship, certain privileges automatically belong to you. Problems arise however, when you either don't know what those privileges are, you don't believe you have them, or you don't believe you're worthy of said privileges.

I am a Princess who never knew it. My behaviors absolutely proved I didn't get it. I was striving for the love, acceptance and status that was already mine. I was in a pointless battle because I was already the winner. I had a relationship with God but I didn't truly understand who God was or who He created me to be. I knew some scriptures. I had many prophetic words spoken over my life and that gave me levels of encouragement and success. However, what I've come to understand is that I needed more than some familiarity with a few scriptures. I needed to know the truth about the nature of God, and about who I am and what I have in Him and then wholeheartedly believe it. Believing is key. Belief will drive your actions, interactions and reactions; these are the very things that will determine your ability to get and stay on your path to purpose.

There is no time like NOW to embrace the woman God destined for you to be. It takes courage to be YOU! Originally RED® is all about being brave enough to be the woman God originally created you to be. I say brave because, often in order to uncover that woman, some deep pains, disappointments, sins, etc. need to be confronted and dealt with. That's not an easy process. Many jump ship before the work is done and continue walking around broken, wounded, and living behind walls and defense mechanisms. Their beautiful Originally RED® identity is hidden. Don't let this be your story. There is no time like NOW to unveil the woman God destined for you to be. Be Originally RED®. Be Bold. Be Brave. Be You!

I pray that as you read this book you would recognize your true worth. I pray truth will shatter every lie that has hindered you from walking in the fullness of the call of God on your life. I pray every wound that has caused you to wear masks of protection would be revealed and healed. I pray that you would come away believing your voice has the power to shift atmospheres and the courage to use it to pass that on to the generation of girls following behind you.

RED REVELATION

I remember the day like it was yesterday. One of my dearest friends and both of our sisters rented a beach house for my 28th birthday. We were all living in different states. I arrived to the beach house first and started watching an episode of *What Not to Wear* while I waited for the girls to arrive. Now, before I go on, you need to know this tidbit. I hated the color red. I refused to wear it. I didn't wear most colors. My wardrobe consisted of various shades of black and gray with the occasional color thrown in and my clothes were often too big. Back to my story. Host of What Not to Wear, Stacy London was speaking to a woman about why she wouldn't wear the color red. Stacy told the woman that not only should she wear red but she deserved to wear red. Stacy went on to say that RED causes you to stand out. When you walk into a room wearing RED, you command attention. RED is loud and bold. A woman who wears RED is confident.

I was staring at the T.V., having an 'aha' moment. As I listened to Stacy London, I realized all the characteristics she listed of women who wear red were things I typically avoided. I had been hiding for years. My lack of wearing colors and oversized clothing was a symptom of something deeper. I was hiding my brilliance. I was hiding my gifts and talents. I was hiding from who I was created to be. I was hiding my identity and running from purpose. I started wearing RED and never looked back. I wanted to be the RED wearing woman Stacy was describing. I wanted to be a "RED". I wanted to command attention. I wanted to be confident. I wanted to be bold. I wanted these things not so people would notice me but so the message God has given me could truly be heard, seen, and felt around the world to bring life transformation. There was no way for me to know fully what that message was because I was too busy keeping up my walls of protection to discover what it could be.

All of a sudden RED was no longer my dreaded color. I didn't go out and buy a RED dress but God did begin to use the color to speak to me. I bought red accessories. I now have beloved red heels and boots! NEVER would I have worn any of this before. Red became part of my brand, SimplicitybyNicole.com. God began to use ladybugs to confirm things to me on a regular basis. God was using a lesson from a T.V. show to make a major life transforming point in my life. I was not created to hide. I was not created to be silent. I was not created to be overlooked. I was not created to settle. I was not created to accept crumbs. I was not created to be used up and tossed aside. I was created to be the leading lady in my life. I was originally intended to be a "RED". So were YOU. God intended every woman to be a "RED" in her own way. It's not about the color RED per se. It's about being fully confident in the woman you are and the purpose in which you are called to walk. It sounds simple but can be a major challenge when the trials of life begin happening before we are truly resigned to the truths in God's word. This was only the beginning of a deeper journey with the Lord. You see, I was already 28 when I was just starting to get it. Lots of life had been lived. Lots of mistakes made. My heart had already suffered greatly. This revelation was the beginning of my process to a healed identity. It's been ten years since my RED Revelation. I'm still fighting to get it. I'm still fighting to become her: the woman God originally intended me to be....RED. The difference now is that I'm fighting armed with truth and knowledge. Now my fight is to let those truths be my guiding force. No longer am I fighting for acceptance and validation that I already possess. I'm inviting you on this journey with me so that together we make the journey easier for our baby girls.

I was scrolling through my Facebook newsfeed one day and I was struck by this overwhelming sadness. I was reading posts from young women ranging from high school through late 20's. Their words were so sad. Their pain was evident. The emptiness they felt was abundantly clear. The photos they posted of themselves were gorgeous yet the

words they wrote about their pictures were de-
meaning. My heart sunk as I picked out certain
pages to read further. Their attempts in obtaining
attention were heartbreaking and only deepened
what I already knew. Our girls are in trouble and
they are crying out for help. Their cries for help often make us angry. We tend to judge them instead
of recognizing the greater problem. I see these girls
being judged and talked about in the news and on
social media regularly. Many of these judgmental
comments come from women. I believe the criticism of these young ladies comes strongly from us
because their behaviors hit a familiar place inside of
us. I knew I needed to do something to pour into a
generation of young women so they didn't become a
generation of wounded women unable to fully func-
tion in purpose. I started to do some research.

I sat down and emailed some of the fabulous
women in my circle and asked them what they
would tell their 18-year-old selves about identity
and purpose. As their answers started to flood my
inbox, I started weeping over my laptop. Their
words were piercing my heart as if they were speaking directly to me. Suddenly, I realized that's exactly
what they were doing. I asked my friends to speak
to the hearts of teenage women. As they did that,
what happened was pain, wounds, and emptiness in
my adult heart that had been there for years were
being ministered to. I understood in that moment,
the best way for me to impact young women was to

help bring awareness and healing to their mothers, grandmothers, aunts, and mentors: that would be you. They follow our lead. We can't impart to them what we do not have. If we do not believe in our value, worth, and undeniable purpose, how can we ever guide them into discovery of these things for themselves. I'll get to some of the amazing responses I received later on but first, go with me on a journey.

Confessions of a Lost RED

"Every temptation is an attempt by the devil to get us to live our lives independently of God. Satan tempts us just as he did Jesus by appealing to our most basic and legitimate needs. The question is: Are these needs going to be met by the world, the flesh and the devil, or are they going to be met by God who promises to meet all our needs 'according to His riches in glory in Christ Jesus' (Phil 4:19)? The most critical needs are the being needs and they are most wonderfully met in Christ."- Neil T. Anderson in Victory over the Darkness

"The being needs." I have struggled greatly with these. I was broken. I was lost. I tried to meet my "being needs", which are legitimate needs, in worldly, fleshly ways when they can only be truly met in

Christ. The need to be loved, accepted, secure, significant, valued, and worthy are deep within all of us. Trying to meet being needs in anything other than Christ causes you to act outside of your true identity. I know this from experience.

I found myself in precarious situations trying to meet my being needs on my own. One situation stands out vividly. It was full of emotion and pain. It was full of revelation about what I truly believe about myself and God. On my journey through this situation, I took the time to see myself, I mean really allowed God to illuminate some things for me. It was one of the most heart-wrenching seasons of my life. It wasn't because God is hurtful or mean. He has been kind and gracious through it all. It was because I thought I conquered this particular struggle and insecurity. I'm sure many of you can relate to thinking you had overcome in an area only to find there was more healing available to you. I had overcome a great deal and I thought I was fully confident and walking as a RED. I was slapped awake to the reality that I clearly was not. God allowed me to see that not only was it not conquered, but He was going to use me as a voice to help other women. One of the reasons I'm alive is to help you become a RED. The more women who get the revelation to live as REDs, the more impact we will have on our girls. The mistakes I have made and the lessons I learned from them are key. Let's start with the mistakes made and see if any of these sound familiar to you (whether done by you or a woman you know).

1. I tried to meet my needs in my own way (consciously and subconsciously)
2. I was flattered by the flirting of men who were clearly not for me to the point that I came to want, need, and expect it.
3. I allowed myself to be put in compromising situations because I was lonely and just wanted to be loved, even though logically I knew there was no way I could be satisfied from these connections.
4. Instead of turning to God for comfort, I turned to men who loved to listen to me, cared about me and tried to help me, but were not available to me emotionally or because they "belonged" to someone else.
5. I ended up developing deep feelings for men who were not for me because I was hurting, lonely, and tired of waiting. I was not focused on God or trusting Him with promises He had spoken over my life.

The aftermath of these mistakes:

The following are excerpts from my journal after the realization that I was still struggling with identity, worth, and value. As you read, you can see God walking me through some important lessons.

"God, I'm so sorry I allowed loneliness and emptiness of heart to put me in situations like this one."

".....God, I have to let go of jealousy. I have to stay focused on the fact that you have a man for me. I do not have to be jealous because you have something beautiful for me. I'm excited. I know you love me God. You are so kind. You are so good. You're loving. You adore me. You have plans for me. They include an amazing man of God. Thank you God that I have right relationships in all areas of my life. Thank you God that I keep healthy boundaries in all areas of my life."

"The painful thing about all of this is my heart now has to go through the process of healing. I've been operating in a lot of fear. I was too afraid to be honest and draw appropriate boundaries that I let way too many inappropriate feelings develop. I was overcome with loneliness and struggling to trust God with my future."

"I do not like the fact that I was so empty and lacking in the knowledge of God's love for me that I allowed myself to fall for someone who clearly is not for me, again. I need to move past this and rest in my God. I'm so angry this happened but now I need to give my

heart the space and time to heal. I have to train my brain to align with You, your word and what you are saying to me in this hour." I had this quote written, "When your daily decisions are aligned with your vision, you create the life you want."

"The cry of my heart today God is to be with you. I know you are always with me but I am not always with you...meaning I'm not always living from a place of awareness of your presence, power and love for me. God, I recognize this time in my life as a time of healing, purging, discovering and building."

Can you feel the pain as you read my words? It is a painful thing when we find ourselves out of alignment with who God says we are and where He wants us to be. It can cause havoc in our lives and those we are connected to. Then we have to go through a healing process with the Lord. Typically, that involves a great deal of pain. It's pain with purpose but still pain nonetheless. I wanted to share the raw feelings from my journey because I think it's important to understand that you are not alone. Our experiences may not be the same. However, most of us have been in situations that cause us to feel what I was expressing in my journal entries. One thing the enemy loves to do is isolate us in our experience, sin, and pain making us believe no one can relate or that we're the biggest failure or sinner around. That is a huge barrier to healing.

As you reading my journal entries, you can see the valuable lessons God walked me through during my healing process. Honestly, none of them were new revelations to me and they may not be to you either. Healing often happens in stages though. At that particular time in my life, God was going to the very core in issues of security, rejection, and identity that I had dealt with numerous times. This time it was sinking into my spirit in a way it hadn't previously. Here are some of those lessons.

- Affirmation must be found in God and God alone. When you look to man to affirm and validate you, you will be disappointed and hurt.

- God will never leave you or forsake you. You are never alone. I learned that God is faithful, kind, and patient. Even though I struggled with certain issues repeatedly, He didn't say, "Forget it! Forget her." He never gave up on me. He patiently walked me through a process of knowing Him at deeper and deeper levels, which then revealed my true essence.

- Boundaries are critical. Boundaries are created for protection. When put in place

properly, they allow the appropriate connections to flow and the inappropriate
connections to cease. Ask God to illuminate your mind on how to set proper
boundaries.

- You need an experiential knowledge of
  who God is and His love for you to operate
  correctly in relationships. You need more
  than a familiarity with God. You need a
  sustained, intimately God-focused relationship. If you don't have this, don't
  despair. Ask God to help you. He will meet
  you right where you are and help you get
  where you need to be. This is important
  because when the emptiness of your heart
  is not filled with Jesus's presence, you will
  fill it with things not of God. Remember
  "not of God" does not necessarily mean
  bad. It means you will use something other than the presence of God to meet the
  deep needs we all have.

- You must think about what you're thinking about. I was thinking about men and
  how they made me feel comforted and accepted rather than recognizing that I am
  already accepted and chosen. Therefore, I
  don't have to fall into situations not of
  God to be validated. Isaiah 26:3 says, "You
  keep him in perfect peace whose mind is

stayed on you because he trusts in You." I was not in peace. My mind wasn't on God. My mind was on pain, disappointment, rejection, and fear. I acted out of that.

- Messiness that we create because of our faults and unmet needs does not disqualify us from the message our lives were destined to speak. If you take the mess to God and allow Him to clean it up, it can then become your message. Let that sink in- your mess can become your message.

I know enough women to know that I'm not alone. Many of us have fallen into relationships that have been out of the will of God. We do this because we're searching for something. We're trying to fill unmet needs. Unfortunately, as daughters of the King, we're searching in the wrong places for something we already possess, our RED identity. I was a lost RED. My Originally RED® identity was covered up by so much pain, disappointment and rejection. It was relatively easy for me to fall into the same cycle repeatedly.

My example of being a lost RED is about relationships with men. That's for one main reason. It is the main area I see our young girls struggling with most when it comes to identity, worth, and purpose. They post pictures of themselves scantily dressed. Why? It gets them attention from boys.

They post negative comments about their appearance and bodies. Why? They hope boys will respond to the contrary. Girls are in abusive relationships at alarming rates. Why? To many girls, any attention is better than no attention, and if he is jealous or angry, that means he cares. They rationalize sexual acts as being ok because they're "not really sex." Some don't even feel the need to rationalize. They'll do whatever they need to do to experience the moments of affirmation, validation, and acceptance they crave. I've been there in one way or another repeatedly over the years. I'm sure many of you have been as well. The sad thing is many of you still are. It's just that our means and methods are usually different now that we're older.

Our girls are crying out to be seen, heard, loved, validated, and affirmed. They are "RED" and they don't know it. Who is going to show them by confidently walking out their REDness? Who will be bold enough? Who will be brave enough? Who will be submitted and honest enough to allow God to do the work in you to bring about your REDness? Will you?

Your issues with identity may not materialize in a way that relates to men. There are many other areas of life that hold women back because they are stuck in insecurities, pain and wrong beliefs about who they are and how much they are loved. Maybe it's in business or professional relationships. You do not have to say yes to every opportunity that comes your way because you are afraid to say no. Not every business opportunity or connection is for you and that is ok. Even if the person is a friend of yours, it is ok to say no if the answer is truly supposed to be no. You actually need to say no because the consequences of saying yes to something meant to be a no are much heavier than the slight and temporary discomfort of your no. Women, we get stuck here quite often. I absolutely know from experience. We get stuck because somewhere along the way, we started believing our "YES" was needed for us to be liked, loved, and accepted. We started believing what we wanted and needed was not as important as the needs and wants of others. Your voice, your purpose, your direction matter. Own that. Believe that. You are somebody. These are not vain statements. These statements are a reality because of the blood of Jesus and your standing in the Kingdom of God. He died for you and filled you with great purpose. You must be able to discern who and what you should be connected to and be bold enough to make decisions aligning with those truths.

Just as you can't say yes to all things, you cannot continue to say no because of fear, resentment, or feelings of unworthiness. I lived in this place for too long. This year, I turn 38. I have never been married. I have never had children. Those two sentences used to grieve my heart deeply. In my

20's and early 30's, God had me on an interesting journey. Every single position I worked in dealt with children. I love children. They are authentic, unjaded and unscarred by life. Not only was I trained to work with them, I found that children were naturally drawn to me. I'm great with them. I love them. They love me. In addition to that, I found myself deeply involved in the marriages of several sets of friends who all happened to be going through insanely difficult times. I was involved as a support, mediator, counselor to the wives and kiddos, etc. As a single person, my eyes were opened to the realities of marriage I'm not sure most single people have the opportunity to witness. People started asking me for advice. That's right. People wanted advice from me the "non-Mom" on what to do with their children. They wanted advice from me the, single girl, on how to handle situations in their marriages. I was overwhelmed. I shut down often. The words, "You are not a wife and you are not a mom, you have no right to speak on these top- ics," played over and over in my mind. The answer in my heart was a resounding NO. My no did not stop people from asking. It also did not stop the training of life experience from happening. I grew to resent it. I was fearful. I resented being asked to help families when all I wanted was to start my own. I was angry it hadn't happened yet. I was fear- ful I would be judged for speaking on something I didn't have direct experience in.

One day a very good friend of mine called me on this. She said, "I know you have something to say about my marriage. You need to open your mouth and speak what God is saying to you." She was correct. I did have something to say about it but I was scared and insecure about it. Who was I to speak on her marriage? The same has happened with children. I've had Moms ask me to come observe their families and then tell them what they're doing wrong (kind of like Supernanny). Though I'm not a wife or a mom yet, God has put me in situations that have given me a great deal of wisdom on how to go about things. I've dealt with more children and families on an intimate level than most people ever will simply because of my work and the call of God on my life in this area. I was allowing my voice to be silenced because of insecurities. We fall into this trap often and it keeps us from fulfilling all God is calling us to do. If God could use a donkey to speak to Balaam (Numbers 22), then He can certainly use me to bring truth, healing, and deliverance regardless of my marital status.

He can use you too! You have a voice. You have a purpose. You matter. I don't care whether you are a stay at home Mom or a corporate executive. It doesn't matter whether you have multiple higher level degrees or a GED. Your status as married or single is irrelevant. You have value because you are a daughter of The King. This is the recurring theme throughout this book. I hope everyone who reads this will experience the Aha Moment they need to shift them into action. As you embrace the truth of who God says you are and live from a place of worth and acceptance, you gain the ability to make lasting impact in the Kingdom of God.

God intends to use women for great and mighty purposes. You see examples of this throughout the Bible as you read the stories of Rahab, Esther, Deborah, Jael, Naomi, Ruth, and Mary to name a few. You too have great purpose that was established by God before you were born. This is why it breaks my heart when I hear women say, they can't start moving in purpose until their husband comes along. What? This is a terrible trick of the enemy to silence our voices. I never thought I had been tricked this way. God recently showed me the subtle way I had been.

I'm an entrepreneur. This is nothing I ever wanted for myself. Trust me, I would've been happy to have my Guidance Counseling job, my hubby, three kids and my white picket fence. God had other ideas though. I've been on a journey with Him in the direction of entrepreneurship since 2002. I was trying to decide on a business name. I wanted my first name, Nicole, in the name but I refused to put my last name, Pertillar anywhere. I came up with a name I was happy with and have been growing that brand for years. Recently, I was reading a book intended to help me with marketing my first book and all of a sudden it hit me. I was not allowing the fullness of who God created me to be in the way I had set up my business. God told me to buy NicoleMichellePertillar.com and I did. Once I did that, so many things started to make sense about the direction God was taking me and who I was to become in business and ministry. I hadn't wanted my maiden name to be in my brand at all. I am not saying you must use your maiden name on any businesses you build or books you write before getting married. This was more of a heart issue for me. I was focused on what I felt my future in business and ministry would look like with my husband because of the vision God had given me. However, I don't become whole and ready to impact the Kingdom of God when I become a Mrs. Just like you, I was whole and ready to impact the Kingdom of God when I accepted Jesus as my Lord and Savior but my focus on the fact that I was not married was holding me back. God's purpose and vision was implanted in my spirit before I was born. I'm still not married but my voice in the Kingdom of God is being solidified independently from that of my husbands because I am a whole individual. This does not mean, I will not work side by side with my husband in business and ministry like I've envisioned. It means I now have clear direction for the path God has me on and that man will be able to find me because I'll look like his missing part as I walk in what God has for me to do. You see, God created Eve for Adam. God took a piece of Adam's body, his rib, and created Eve for him. Eve was complete when God created her. She was the original Originally RED® woman. It was only when Eve stepped outside of what God originally intended for her that trouble began.

Single ladies, God has given you a voice and a purpose. Don't wait. Be brave. Be bold. Go after it now before your man finds you. Let God show you all He has for you from a place of intimacy with Him. Then teach the girls God blesses you to influence how to do the same thing from a young age so they don't have to go through the deep processes of healing that you and I have and continue to walk through.

Married ladies, God has given you a voice and a purpose. If you feel empty, lonely, and tired even in the midst of your marriage sometimes, turn to God and let Him fill you. Let Him show you the RED woman He originally created you to be. You are a gift to your husband. That gift is at its absolute best when you know your value, worth, and purpose. Accept it, believe it, and walk in it. Let your REDness shine brightly so that as you live from a place of authenticity and wholeness in Jesus, you can be an example to the girls God gives you in your sphere of influence.

Do you see the theme?

- We are all RED and we all need to own it. Marital status has nothing to do with it.
- All of us have girls and young women in our spheres of influence whether we are raising them or not.
- This will not change. This is the way God originally intended it.

We're all in different stages of the same journey. To effectively impact the next generation, we must be solid in knowing who we are as HIS and boldly embrace our authentic identity.

1. Meditate on 2 Corinthians 3:16-18. Write it out below.

_____

_____

_____

_____

_____

2. What was Nicole's RED Revelation (aha moment)?

_____

_____

_____

_____

_____

_____
_____

3. Describe any aha moments you've had that have helped you move toward living a more authentic life (your original identity).

_____
_____
_____
_____
_____

4. What does it mean to be a RED woman?

_____
_____
_____
_____
_____

5. What are the most critical needs we have and what are some examples of those needs?

_____
_____
_____
_____
_____
_____

6. What are some mistakes you recognize in your life from trying to meet your needs without Christ?

_____

_____

_____

_____

_____

_____

7. What does it mean to be a lost RED? Do you feel you are or have been a lost RED? Explain.

_____

_____

_____

_____

_____

_____

_____

_____

_____

_____

8. Do you recognize issues of identity in your life? What are they?

_____

_____

_____

_____

_____

RED IDENTITY

I touched on what it means to be a RED briefly when talking about my RED Revelation. Let's dig a bit deeper though. Remember, I talked about being princesses because we are daughters of The King? Now, don't get caught up on preconceived ideas of what it means to be a princess. There are princesses who love lace, frilly things, and tea parties. There are also princesses who love Nikes and football. This is not about that. As daughters of the King, we have royal standing. We have royal identity. We have been chosen to receive all our Father has simply because we are HIS. Do you know that? Do you believe that? Do you understand what that even means? I don't think most of us do because if we did, we'd be so much more powerful in the Kingdom of God than what we display on a daily basis. They are not just words on paper. They are our reality as daughters of God. However, because of sin (ours and the sins of others toward us) we have not been able to live in that reality. When we don't live out of our identity as daughters of The King, we are living out of identities as orphans.

We all know an orphan is a child without parents. When we are not rightly aligned as princesses

of The King, essentially we are orphans and we operate out of an orphan spirit. Regardless of how we
were raised in our families of origin, I believe all of
us experience orphan spirit tendencies before we
are adopted into the Kingdom of God. However,
even after we've been adopted by God, as evidenced
by my life, we can struggle with an orphan spirit.
How do you know you have an orphan spirit? This
quote by the late Jack Frost, who was a champion of
teaching on the Father's Heart explains it quite
well.

> *"The orphan spirit causes one to live life as if
> he does not have a safe and secure place in
> the Father's heart. He feels he has no place of
> affirmation, protection, comfort, belonging,
> or affection. Self-oriented, lonely, and in-
> wardly isolated, he has no one from whom to
> draw Godly inheritance. Therefore, he has to
> strive, achieve, compete, and earn everything
> he gets in life. It easily leads to a life of anxie-
> ty, fears, and frustration." –Jack Frost*

I see this spirit running rampant among young
girls. You can see evidence of this at younger and
younger ages as you watch girls interact with each
other, boys, and the way they view themselves. Dare
I say, our girls are suffering from an orphan spirit
epidemic? It is occurring for girls in and outside of
the church. I also recognize how this spirit has been
operating in me and women I know at varying levels. When operating in the orphan spirit, there is no

way to walk effectively in purpose or help anyone understand their true standing as daughters. The orphan spirit dims our REDness.

The following chart originated from Shiloh Place which is a ministry of the late Jack Frost. It gives an excellent breakdown of some areas of concern when dealing with an orphan spirit in comparison to sonship (adoption as daughters).

You can find the original chart here: ShilohPlace.org

THE HEART OF AN ORPHAN		THE HEART OF SONSHIP
See God as Master	IMAGE OF GOD	See God as a loving Father
Independent/Self-reliant	DEPENDENCY	Interdependent/ Acknowledges Need
Live by the love of law	THEOLOGY	Live by the Law of Love
Insecure/Lack Peace	SECURITY	Rest and Peace
Strive for the praise, approval and acceptance of man	NEED FOR APPROVAL	Totally accepted in God's love and justified by grace
A need for personal achievement as you seek to impress God and others, or no motivation to serve at all	MOTIVE FOR SERVICE	Service that is motivated by a deep gratitude for being unconditionally loved and accepted by God
Duty and earning God's favor or no motivation at all	MOTIVE BEHIND CHRISTIAN	Pleasure and delight

	DISCIPLINES	
"Must" be holy to have God's favor, thus increasing a sense of shame and guilt	MOTIVE FOR PURITY	"Want to" be holy; do not want anything to hinder intimate relationship with God
Self-rejection from comparing yourself to others	SELF-IMAGE	Positive and affirmed because you know you have such value to God
Seek comfort in counterfeit affections: addictions, compulsions, escapism, busyness, hyper-religious activity	SOURCE OF COMFORT	Seek times of quietness and solitude to rest in the Father's presence and love
Competition, rivalry, and jealousy toward others' success and position	PEER RELATIONSHIPS	Humility and unity as you value others and are able to rejoice in their blessings and success
Accusation and exposure in order to make yourself look good by making others look bad	HANDLING OTHERS' FAULTS	Love covers as you seek to restore others in a spirit of love and gentleness
Accusation and exposure in order to make yourself look good by making others look bad	VIEW OF AUTHORITY	Respectful, honoring; you see them as ministers of God for good in your life
See authority as a source of pain; distrustful toward them and lack a heart attitude of submission	VIEW OF ADMONITION	See the receiving of admonition as a blessing and need in your life so that your faults and weaknesses are exposed and put

		to death
Difficulty receiving admonition; you must be right so you easily get your feelings hurt and close your spirit to discipline	EXPRESSION OF LOVE	Open, patient, and affectionate as you lay your life and agendas down in order to meet the needs of others
Guarded and conditional; based upon others' performance as you seek to get your own needs met	SENSE OF GOD'S PRESENSE	Open, patient, and affectionate as you lay your life and agendas down in order to meet the needs of others
Bondage	CONDITION	Liberty
Spiritual ambition; the earnest desire for some spiritual achievement and distinction and the willingness to strive for it; a desire to be seen and counted among the mature.	VISION	To daily experience the Father's unconditional love and acceptance and then be sent as a representative of His love to family and others.
Fight for what you can get!	FUTURE	Sonship releases your inheritance!

Each time I go over this chart, the areas I have struggled in are abundantly clear. Here I am almost 38 years old and just coming to an understanding of my standing as the daughter of The King. Take an honest inventory of your heart. Do you recognize characteristics of an orphan in yourself? The orphan spirit covers up your Original RED® identity.

Zari Banks, who can be found at zaribanks.co, is someone I consider a mentor in the area of adoption as sons and daughters. She has an amazing video teaching, called Adopted, that addresses the issue of the orphan spirit. Her teaching is one of the tools God has used to get me more aligned with my Originally RED® identity. Here's a bit of what I've learned from Zari regarding the orphan spirit.

From Zari's Adopted teaching, I learned 5 main reasons we still struggle with the orphan spirit even after we've acknowledged Jesus.

1. Sin
2. Family of Origin
3. Lack of Knowledge
4. Generational Curses
5. Misplaced Worship (Focus)

I'm not going to go into detail on these as Zari does an excellent job teaching what God gave her. I suggest going to her site to order her teaching called "Adopted" for further study, especially if you see yourself in any of the orphan spirit description from the chart. I know the issues I had with identity, worth, value, and purpose entered my life due to all five of the areas Zari mentions in varying levels.

Zari then went on to teach about God as our father and protector. Galatians 4:4-5 speaks about receiving a spirit of adoption. Adoption is our inheritance. Remember, we are princesses, daughters of The King and with that come certain privileges.

1. Acceptance
2. Provision
3. Health and Life
4. Love
5. Spiritual Gifts
6. Access to the heavenlies

Women who walk in all of the above are RED women. Women who understand their inheritance can stand boldly and walk confidently. They can trust the timing of God with His promises because they understand He loves them deeply and knows exactly what they need. RED women understand they are accepted. They do not look to counterfeit affections or strive for the approval of man. They are at peace and rest in the knowledge of their God. They've been transformed by experiencing the Love of their Father. That is a RED identity woman. That is who God originally intended for us to be. Though many of us have lived outside of that identity, it is still there waiting for us to grab hold of it. Are you ready? Originally RED® women are women who have experienced the transformational love of their father, are aware of and walk in their inheritance, and desire greatly to leave their mark in the Kingdom of God. Are you Originally RED®?

In addition to understanding our identity as daughters, another critical piece to walking out an Originally RED® life is being able to forgive. God's word is clear about how necessary it is to forgive.

"And whenever you stand praying, forgive, if you have anything against anyone, so that your Father also who is in heaven may forgive you your trespasses." Mark 11:25(ESV)

"For if you forgive others their trespasses, your heavenly Father will also forgive you." Matthew 6:14(ESV)

"Therefore, confess your sins to one another and pray for one another, that you may be healed. The prayer of a righteous person has great power as it is working." James 5:16(ESV)

Unforgiveness blocks your truth. It blocks your ability to receive what God wants to pour out on you. It blocks your ability to believe what He says about you because you are focused on what was done to you by others or what you perceive God did to you. This in no way downplays anything painful you may have walked through. It is to encourage you that you must release those things to the Lord through forgiveness. I had to go back and forgive, in prayer, every man that hurt me, used me, and let me down. I had to forgive my parents and other family members. I had to forgive friends for judging me or not being able to be what I needed in a certain season. As God would bring people and situations up, I would pray through those things and forgive. It's a discipline we need to make a common practice of if we are ever to live freely. We also need to teach young girls to do the same. Life will go much smoother for them if they can get this. They do not have to repeat the same mistakes we made or are making if we are transparent with them about the process and respond to them from a place of love.

A key thing I've learned about forgiveness is that forgiveness is a choice. It's really not a process as many people teach. You choose to forgive but then you walk through a process of healing. You can forgive and still need to heal. This is extremely important to understand for yourself and as you try to assist anyone else along the way. Don't worry about how long it takes. If you stay in tune with what God is speaking to your heart, you will complete the process in His perfect timing.

Forgive. Forgive. Forgive. If you want to be free, forgive. If you want to live authentically, forgive. If you want to be brave and walk boldly as the woman God originally created you to be, forgive. If you do not, you will continue to have walls and blocks hindering your Originally RED® identity. I'm telling you to forgive. However, forgiveness and the healing process that come with it are not always easy. When forgiveness is difficult, you ask your Father God to help you. If you truly want to forgive someone yet you are struggling to do so, reliance on God and trust in His word are what will get you to the place you need to be.

Another critical component to forgiveness is forgiving yourself. As women, we struggle with this. We often beat ourselves up over mistakes we've made more than anyone else ever could or even would. I did this to myself for years. Guilt and shame built up and created a wedge between me and God because I had not forgiven myself for not being perfect. I hadn't forgiven myself for missing the mark. When guilt and shame is on you, it causes you to want to hide. Hiding was a main part of my RED Revelation. God was showing me that I was hiding who He truly created me to be. I could always sense that I was special, important, and valuable but I also knew my flaws. I identified more with my mistakes and flaws than the greatness I had glimmers of and it held me back. Being Originally RED® means you will identify with the woman God has designed you to be. It means you won't allow her to stay quiet and hidden. What do you need to forgive yourself for? Who do you need to forgive?

Reflection Questions:

1. What is an orphan Spirit?

   _____

   _____

   _____

_____

_____

_____

2. What, if any, orphan spirit characteristics do you recognize in your life?

_____

_____

_____

_____

_____

3. If you identified orphan spirit characteristics in your life, are you able to pinpoint how they developed?

_____

_____

_____

_____

_____

_____

4. How does unforgiveness impact a person's ability to live an OriginallyRED® identity?

_____

_____

_____

_____

_____

_____

5. Is there anyone you need to forgive? Who? Why?

_____

_____

_____

_____

_____

_____

6. Have you forgiven yourself?

_____

_____

_____

_____

_____

_____

7. CHALLENGE: Pick 3 categories from the Heart of an Orphan/Heart of Sonship chart that you want to have more success with (i.e. you want to lean toward the heart of Sonship more often than not. Evaluate where you are now and set goals for yourself to get where you would like to be.

_____

_____

_____

_____

_____

RED RESPONSIBILITY

My heart hurts whenever I think about the young girls I know walking through the garbage I've put myself through (and worse) because I didn't understand who I was or who God was. I have often had the thought if I had only known then what I know now life would look so different. I didn't know though. I loved God and knew He loved me. Why didn't I know? I'm sure there are many things that play a role but here are two main reasons. One, I wasn't taught in church. My experience in church during my foundational years was more about making sure I did what was right rather than becoming the woman God created me to be. Secondly, my Mom didn't know. It was later in my life that my Mom understood and started believing many of the fundamental truths that we were familiar with but not fully grasping. She has shared with me that she wished she knew what she knows now when I was growing up so she could have trained my sister and I more effectively and how it will be different for my children. This brings me to the RED Responsibility.

The main thing I want you to get out of this book is healing and freedom. I pray that my experiences open you up to hear from God about your life and areas where you need to walk in greater alignment with who He originally intended you to be. The other thing I want you to take from this is ownership of The RED Responsibility. It's our responsibility as Originally RED® women of God to pour into our peers and the generations coming behind us. I want them to know they are princesses. I want them to know themselves not as Disney princesses, but as Kingdom Princesses; a princess whose Father is the King of Kings. There is no reason why an army of women equipped with the transformational knowledge of their Originally RED® identity as princesses of The King can't go out and train up a radical army of Young Righteous REDs who will enter into adulthood already equipped to fight the battles that wore many of us out!

There is no age too young to start training our girls to be Originally RED® Warriors. We can speak the truth of God's word to them in the womb and even speak life over them prior to their conception by praying and speaking scriptures to them before they're even born. Of course we know that won't happen for every little girl and that is why it's our RED Responsibility to train and equip the young ladies that God puts within our circle of influence. I have a follow up book already in the works that will lay out a plan of how to do this and the importance of doing so. In the meantime though, it starts with you. You have a responsibility to be Originally RED®. You have a responsibility to be the woman

God intended for you to be before all those Daddy wounds from childhood came in, before the abuse occurred, before the deep losses, before the loneliness and emptiness overtook your heart, before lack consumed you, before the man you loved married someone else, before disappointment became routine, before you forgot you do have good ideas, before your marriage ended, before the abortion, before the rape, before you depended on your husband to fill areas of your heart only God could fill, before you lost your joy, and before you were rejected so many times you began to believe there was something wrong with you. Let God show you the woman He destined for you to be before life happened and masks with walls of protection showed up to cover your true identity. Shift your focus from wounds, pains, and lies to the truth that you are whole, valuable worthy and not damaged goods. Then, you will be free. "You will know the truth, and the truth will set you free." (John 8:32)

Once you obtain that freedom, you have to fight to keep it. I believe this is the point where many get tripped up. Often we can get free, but remaining free becomes the challenge. In order to remain free, you must nurture your heart and feed your freedom. What do I mean by feeding your freedom? Just as any other living, breathing, organism must be fed, you must be spiritually fed. After going through a long and intense heart healing process with several layers, I have come to understand I can't be lax about my freedom in Christ. Every aspect of it must be guarded diligently.

How do you feed your freedom? I believe God will give you specific ways to do that for you. We are all different. We all have different situations we're dealing with that may call for specific actions as we come into alignment with who God says we are. However, there are some basic principles that apply to everyone.

Guard your heart. "Above all else, guard your heart, for everything you do flows from it" (Proverbs 4:23 NIV). Everything you do flows from your heart. If your heart is clogged with bitterness, unforgiveness, shame, guilt, etc., how can you do anything in your maximum God-given capacity? Guarding of the heart may look different for different women. However, we all need to do it. Ask God what ways you should be guarding your heart that you aren't currently doing. The following are a few basic steps I've had to take on this journey.

- **Study the word of God.** Hide the word in your heart. "I have hidden your word in my heart that I might not sin against you" (Psalm 119:11 NIV). I know this sounds so basic especially for those who have been saved for a long time. However, how many truly make this a practice? Again, this is not about being familiar with a few scrip-

tures. This is getting intimately acquainted with the word of God so that it spills
out of you. I'm still in process with this
but I stay connected to those who are far-
ther along. I'm not where I want to be
with it but I'm also not where I was and
that's the key to feeding my freedom. At
the end of this book, I've shared with you
some of the scriptures, affirmations, and
books that have helped me to feed my
freedom.

- **Practice the Presence of God.** Times
  of intimate worship to the Lord have fed
  my freedom. There have been times where
  I could do nothing else but say the name
  of Jesus or cry out to Him in worship.
  How many of you know what I mean? I'm
  thankful that the word says God is literally
  in our praise. "Still, You are holy;   You
  make Your home on the praises of Israel"
  (Psalm 22:3 The Voice). In moments of
  weakness, He was strong on my behalf.
  Also, getting in the habit of acknowledging
  God all throughout the day helps im-
  mensely.   He's   always   there   but
  acknowledging Him was the key to break-
  through. Invite His presence into your
  daily grind. Welcome Him to speak to you
  and lead you.

- **Govern Your Circle.** If I could shout this one from the mountaintops I would. You must be vigilant about who gets in your space, who gets your time, your energy, and your ear. I could be wrong but I believe women have the most difficulty with this. This is not to say that men don't ever struggle with it but women, our circles can truly set us back if we're not careful. Do your relationships feed what God is doing in your heart right now? Do your relationships encourage you to be better at whatever it is God has you doing in this season? Do your relationships respect your boundaries? Do they draw you closer to God? If you allow relationships in your inner circle that drain you, use you, lie to you, discourage you, and constantly remind you of who you were and what you did and what you don't have, then you are setting yourself up to stay stuck. Remember, this is not about a friend being a bad person now. This is about a particular friend or relationship that you may need to love from a distance for a season and possibly forever as you walk into all God has for you as the woman He created you to be. Everyone cannot go with you.

- **Protect Your Gates.** When God is healing and revealing things in your life, you cannot fill your eyes and ears with any and everything. Some TV shows you may have always considered harmless entertainment might have to go. Trust me. I know. I've walked through having to let go of TV shows because God told me I could not fill my spirit with them. The same goes for music. I can't listen to all music. Even some music that I truly love is totally off the table now. Why? I'm guarding my freedom. That may seem extreme to some people. What I say to that is, being the woman God created me to be and fulfilling the purpose He birthed in me is extreme. I challenge you to ask yourself if there are areas God wants you to protect more diligently.

God wants to take you on a journey of healing that will inevitably release you to walk in total freedom as His daughter. Maybe you're already on this journey. Maybe you're just starting out. In either case, I want you to fight for your freedom. As you do this, you will be positioned to help shape the lives of other women and young girls who need to walk in freedom.

In chapter 1, I mentioned reaching out to several friends to ask them what they would tell their 18-

year-old selves about identity and purpose. My goal was to develop a tool to assist young girls with understanding identity. I was able to do this because I know my circle. I knew the women I asked would have phenomenal words of wisdom to pour into the lives of young girls. I wept over their words as I received them. I was touched in a deep way. They spoke to pain, disappointments, and mistakes I had carried since childhood. My response to their words helped me determine this book was actually intended for women rather than teenagers. One of the ways I'm called to help those young ladies is to help you - their Moms, Aunts, Grandmothers, Mentors, etc. I pray the words written by my friends will assist you on your own process of becoming and embracing your Original RED® identity. Here are some of the responses that impacted me to my core. The response of my friend is listed followed by a short synopsis by me. I pray you feel the love of God for you as you read.

"I look at you with so much love and compassion because I know exactly what you are going through. I know the pain of trying to find love and trying to prove that you are lovable only to be betrayed, cheated on, cursed out, and abused. I know that for most of your life you have been longing for true friendship and acceptance yet it seems that even when you think you have that, it never lasts.

For now, you are busy trying to prove yourself to someone who can't see beyond his own insecurities. I wish I could convince you of what you already know – that you are not responsible for his fits of rage. You have done nothing wrong, and you know that. You are desperately hoping that you are not wrong about him, so that you won't be wrong about giving yourself to him. Don't worry about that, God will restore you and He won't hold any of it against you. You will walk away from him and it will be so easy, you will wonder why you didn't do it sooner. It's as easy as making the decision to cut ties and asking your parents for support in your decision.

I know- that probably seems like the last thing you would want to do – go to your parents. They seem very harsh at times but I can assure you that you are so precious to them and they are more proud of you than you could even understand right now. They come across the way they do because they worry about you. They want to protect you but they can't stop you from making your own decisions.

You should know that your intense desire to find love and acceptance will always lead you into traps of hurt and betrayal when you expect people to fulfill those desires. The abuse will not end here but will be a recurring theme in different ways with different guys as long as you cling to the idea that the right "relationship" will fix it. There is no man who will fix it for you. There is nothing you can do to make yourself so pleasing to a man that he will love you the way you desire to be loved. God has designed your life in such a way that it will not work unless you are firmly grounded in Him, clinging to Him for love and acceptance. It is only when we submit ourselves to this, that we find true love and happiness.

Your true identity has been hidden from you for so long. You have seen glimpses of it in your dreams though. God will use you mightily to minister to His people, to help them fulfill their goals and dreams, and lead them back to Him. Your writing will open many doors for you – I know this can be hard to conceive of, but it is true.

Learn that God is your source for everything – in love, relationships, finances, your career, everything. Keep talking to God, keep writing to Him in your journals – He loves that. You are so special to Him and He has such great plans for you. The more you grow in relationship with Him, the more He will reveal Himself to you and the more clearly you will hear Him. If a relationship or activity seems to hinder your spiritual growth, that is a sure sign that it has no place in your life. Seek God's approval first so you can avoid heartache.

One last thing, and this is perhaps most important. You will make mistakes. Everyone does, but you tend to be extremely hard on yourself. You also have a notion that God is disappointed with you because of the things you struggle with. That is a trick of the enemy to make you hide yourself in shame, just like Adam and Eve did in the Garden of Eden. Surprise the enemy and surprise yourself. When you mess up, run straight to God, straight into His arms. Talk to Him honestly about what happened. Repent and allow Him to comfort you. God does not hold grudges or give you the cold shoulder like people do. Run to Him no matter what. He is always there for you.

I love you for who you are, a beautifully, wonderfully made daughter of the King."

~Rachel Renee, Author, Ghostwriter, RachelRenee.live, RainPublishing.com, dear friend and ministry partner.

These eloquent words from my dear friend Rachel still bring tears to my eyes. Rachel speaks directly to struggles I have faced. As I read her words, I recognized how often I didn't do what she said: run to God. I did what she said not to do. I intensely looked for love which led me into many traps and caused great heartache. My prayer for you is that no matter what mistakes you have made in your life, you will understand that God is always there for you. He is not angry at you. There is grace and forgiveness for every error we make. Rest with that knowledge and let the reality of that kind of love spur you to continually run to the Lord. He is kind and it is His kindness that leads us to repentance (Romans 2:4).

As you think about pouring into the next generation, remember there is no need to come at them with fear and control. Yes, we desperately want them to skip the heartache many of us have experienced. The way to do that is to show them the truth of who they are, providing an environment of peace and acceptance and living a bold, brave Originally RED® life.

"I would love to tell my 18 year old self that you do not have to have your life planned at 18. It is good to have a plan, but do not be so fixed on that plan where you cannot adapt if something spoils your plan. God may have a completely different path for you. Do not waste all of your life planning your life when you can be living life.

You are more than the label in your clothes, the car you drive, and the house in which you live. So many young girls get their identity from the labels they wear. They forget that God does not care about that. As God's children we are called to be different.

You cannot be all things to all people, so just be yourself. Some people will like you and others may not. Do not waste your time trying to impress people that have nothing to do with your destiny. If you are having trouble finding out who you are, spend some time with our Lord. Most of the time you cannot find yourself when you are surrounded by a crowd of people. Be still and listen for God to speak to you. You may not understand the message or even agree with the message, but listen for it anyway. You must not fight God for control. Step back and trust that He will lead you in the right direction."

~Amanda Adomatis, dear friend from college

All of this is excellent and quite true but what sticks out to me is the last paragraph. "You cannot be all things to all people, so just be yourself." My heart winces as I read this because I can see little girls as young as 2 and 3 desperately trying to please in order to be accepted and loved. They need women who know deep down who they are to impart truth, identity, and purpose into them early. Can you imagine a generation of girls confident enough to simply be who God created them to be? Imagine if you'd had this confidence back when you were 10 years old. Is there a young girl God put in your life that you can help instill this God confidence in?

"There is a beautiful myth that comes along when we cross from adolescence to adulthood. An unwritten commandment that as you grow in wisdom, age and stature proves itself to be false over and over again. Thou Shalt Not Fail.

At the ripe old knowledgeable-about-everything age of 18, I surely thought that the world was my oyster. Ready to scale mountains, charge oceanic shores and absolutely set this world ablaze. I set out to simply blow the lid off of my potential and prove everyone right. Yes. I was amazing! This gifted and talented AP student walked on clouds and thought that she could walk on water. Armed for the journey with boat loads of bravado, I set a course for the highest heights. Can you hear the trumpets sounding? Close your eyes and you can envision my own personal cavalry. Banners, dancers, flags, perhaps even a 21 gun salute and fireworks. Yes! This young confident soldier marched on towards battle with a men's chorus ringing in between her ears and all the preparation in the world. Do you smell that? It's victory in case you hadn't noticed. Pure, unadulterated victory.

So the very first time that I actually failed that whole cavalry screeched to a halt. Failure? Hadn't been on my list of "to-do's." A little shaken, but not defeated I marched on again and again. Until I failed again and again. Suddenly, I could no longer hear that men's chorus. No flags and dancers. The 21 gun salute deserted me for more noble and valiant soldiers and I was left in a wilderness of defeat. Alone, embarrassed, and full of despair I sunk into depression and disengaged from it all. There I sat under a lonely tree with no shade in the desert absolutely in shock and dismay. I was a failure.

The lesson that I learned was far from what you may think. Of course you learn that failure inevitably happens and is an opportunity for growth. Then there's the understanding that resilience is important should one seek to get through life without a breakdown at every turn. Those are all good. But the lesson I would teach my 18 year old self is that I should have never tried to be perfect in the first place.

Hiding flaws to impress others, always being the good-girl, and striving for man's version of perfection does not pay off. When you ignore the long process of personal refinement in order to gain temporary praise it is the beginnings of the path to destruction. You simply cannot stand up under the weight of feigned superiority when life sends blow after blow the way that it does. This kind of attitude only prompts others to give you the false admiration that your false actions generate and that is a recipe for a false confidence and fast failure. Insecurity, self-contempt and pride absolutely flourish in this environment. Planting these seeds in your life will eventually bring forth a rotten bitter harvest. It is not worth it.

So to my 18 year old self, I'd tell her to remove the mask of perfection and instead adorn one of grace. To accept defeat with courage and tenacity and reject the fear of criticism by faking perfection. Rather, be strong and courageous! Do not be so afraid of the shortcomings in your character that you put a pretty bow on top of a rotten place in your heart just to appease the ones that seek to judge you. Instead, confront the hard things now. Trade the opinion and praise of man for the precepts and character lessons that the Lord encourages. When you do, you will grow in wisdom and stature and that will produce both the favor of God and man. (Luke2:52) Trust me, there will be plenty of mountains to climb and valleys to forge in due time. For now, look to the hills for your help and march on my friend. One surefooted step at a time".

~Krisette Cole Friend, Wife, Mom to 5 Amazing Littles and Blogger at FaithfulSeeds.com and www.faithfulseeds.com

While many of the other messages made me cry, this one made me laugh. In the beginning as Krisette pokes fun at her have-it-all-together, know-it-all attitude, I could so relate. I remember feeling as though I had it all together. I also remember when that false reality crumbled time and time again. I tried to cover it up with that big pretty bow Krisette talked about. However, the dirty, ugly places were still there festering. Oh and the always being the "good girl" thing. That was me, hands down. People even called me goody two shoes. I cringe just thinking about it. What echoes in my mind from reading Krisette's words is, "Confront the hard things now." This is critically important ladies. When God nudges you to deal with something, deal with it. When God lets you in on the fact that you're going in a wrong direction, listen. Be honest with Him about why it's hard for you to obey in this area. There is grace for every failure and mistake. You are not perfect. God knows this. Stop pretending to be by hiding your flaws. Shine God's light on those flaws and get free. We need to be comfortable with our flaws because they make our dependence on God so clear. This is such an important lesson we need to grasp. It takes bravery and boldness to deal with your issues. Can you imagine how difficult it is for a young girl to deal? You are needed. We are needed to walk with them in love as they grow in wisdom throughout their lifetime.

"You are a Diamond. Many often seek diamonds because of their brilliance, beauty, and precious value. My daughter, these same descriptions can be applied to you. The biggest hurdle is for you to believe those words accurately portray your true identity. Just think about it. To find the most precious and rarest of gems there must be a time of unearthing after periods of intense heat and pressure. In other words, opportunities for self-discovery and growth happen at all times. Whether you are in a good place or striving just to survive, invite Holy Spirit to lead you on life's journey. Allow Him to love, comfort, teach, and help you. Ask Him to reveal the intents and purposes of His heart for

you as well as those who are to walk with you in this season. Daily get to know Him and yourself by reading and meditating on the Word, prayer, praise and worship. Treat Him as your closest friend and biggest advocate because He is. Share with Him your most intimate secrets, greatest disappointments and biggest dreams. After all, He knows the plans that He has for you and how to get you to your expected end. He wants you to realize you are His special treasure, so let His Splendor arise in you!"

Malachi 3:16-18, Jeremiah 29: 11-13, Psalm 139:14, Romans 8:28 and Romans 8:31

~Valerie Hall, dear friend and one of my personal prayer warriors--she means business too!

This speaks to the issue at the crux of the matter, belief. Do you believe you are a princess of The King? Ms. Valerie stated, "The biggest hurdle is for you to believe those words accurately portray your true identity." It takes time to discover who you are especially after so many life experiences have covered up who God originally intended for you. My sisters, understand that during the process of healing, there will be times of intense pressure. Move through it under the guidance of the Holy Spirit. Don't jump ship on your voyage to wholeness. Let Him help you. Let Him be your best friend. This is where I went wrong. I knew my loneliness and disappointment more intimately than I knew Jesus because that's where my focus was. It's hard to admit but it's the absolute truth. I believed loneliness and pain rather than what I truly had in my Father God. Recently, God told me He was going to show me aspects of Himself that I've never walked in before but it would require a new level of focus to receive what He wanted to pour out to me. Ms. Val's words remind me of this. You must develop an intimate relationship with the Lord. Everything that you will ever need is in Him. It is out of intimate relationship that identity and purpose is revealed. Whatever season of life you find yourself in; married, single, mother, career woman, entrepreneur, etc. intimacy with the Lord will fuel your belief. Our young girls stop believing in their worth and brilliance at younger and younger ages. They need RED women who understand the importance of belief in truth and how to nurture that belief. Will you be one to encourage them in believing they are princesses of The King? You must first believe it for yourself. Do you? Your behavior is the best indicator of your belief. So, what are you doing?

"Everything about you is designed for the greatness that awaits you! Never allow any moment, failure, or person to define you. Those will all pass away. God's definition of you through Christ and how He has uniquely designed you is all the identity you need. Be at peace in Christ and be at peace with just being you and that will be enough!"

~Felicia Craig AKA "LadyLight," iam-chosen.com, friend and ministry partner

Does anything else even need to be said after, "God's definition of you through Christ and how He has uniquely designed you is all the identity you need"? I didn't get this growing up. There was so much I didn't understand. Yes, I could quote some scriptures about my identity in Christ but I needed more than that. I needed to have true relationship rather than religion. I needed to have intimate relationship with the Lord to fully grasp my identity in Him. I had a journey to learn how to do this that was made much harder once life started happening. I know the same is true for many of you. I encourage you to keep going. Dig deeper. Let God speak His truth about who He originally created you to be. Don't settle for being familiar with a few scriptures. That's not enough to withstand the tests and trials of life. It's certainly not enough to press through into the full destiny the Lord has for you. Get intimately acquainted with the Lord. I liken it to the beginning stages of a dating relationship. You are constantly talking to each other. You want to know and understand everything about them. You want them to know you, love you and accept you. Do this with the Lord and you will certainly be Originally RED®. Wouldn't it be wonderful for all of us to get this to the point that we are able to teach all the girls in our sphere of influence how to do this at young ages?

"I would tell my 18-year-old self that self-discovery never ends. Who you are at 18 is not who you will be at 21, nor at 25, 30, 40 and beyond. We continue to grow and explore throughout life SO...don't be in a rush and don't put too much pressure on yourself to figure it all out."

~Kamryn Adams Author, Life Coach- Alliance Life Management and the Kamryn Adams Group, LLC

Lord knows I wish I had grasped this concept back in the day. It would've saved me a great deal of heartache. The reality is, this is one of those lessons that is difficult to internalize unless you've lived a little. However, if all of us can remember this as adults and embrace it as a positive reality of life rather than a detriment, it will be much easier for us to walk in who we are. It will also be much easier for us to support girls as they walk through their process of self-discovery.

My friends covered so much in their responses to the question I posed, "What would you tell your 18-year-old self about identity and purpose?" This is what I would add:

You are a masterpiece, a fine work of art created by the Master Artist. Everything about you was fashioned by His hand. He takes delight in all the aspects of your personality even those you don't like. He loves all of you. As you grow in Him and surrender to what He wants to do in you, He will refine everything about you. Don't stop the process. Yes, sometimes it's hard but it's always harder to jump back in after you stop. So don't stop.

You will encounter many challenging and heartbreaking situations in life. They will not break you. Get God's perspective on everything you walk through. What you think about your situations has more power over you than the situations themselves.

Guard your heart. Focus on all you have in Jesus and what He empowers you to do rather than what you think you can't do or can't have because of being a Christian. No matter what comes your way, remember to do these things: Believe God is who He says He is. Believe God can do what He says He's going to do. Believe you are who God says you are and don't let anyone tell you any differently. To do these things, you must make it a priority to be a student, friend, and daughter of God. A student studies to learn so they can follow the steps of their teacher. A friend gets to know your secrets and God will surely let you in on secrets so you can move in wisdom and discernment. A daughter has access to everything her father has. She is covered, protected, provided for and deeply loved.

You are chosen for a purpose. Your voice matters. Don't let insecurities silence you. Be Bold. Brave. Be You!

~Nicole Michelle Pertillar

1. What is the RED Responsibility?

   _____
   _____
   _____
   _____
   _____
   _____

2. What does it mean to feed your freedom and why is this important?

   _____
   _____
   _____
   _____
   _____
   _____
   _____

3. What are the four ways listed to guard
    your heart? What are other specific ways
    God has given you to protect your heart?

    _____

    _____

    _____

    _____

    _____

    _____

4. What are some lessons you have learned
    that you wish you would have known as a
    young girl?

    _____

    _____

    _____

    _____

    _____

    _____

5. Ask God to highlight at least one girl He
    has for you to pour into and mentor that
    you don't already work with.

    _____

    _____

    _____

    _____

    _____

    _____

RED CHALLENGE

There is a process to becoming Originally RED®, especially after a lifetime of behaviors, relationships and choices cover up your true identity. It does not happen overnight. I'm not sure if on this side of heaven we will ever fully walk in who God created us to be at all times. However, we can have much better than what we've been experiencing. It is time for a generation of women to rise up and be champions of consistent intimate relationship with Jesus. It's from that place that everything changes. When you establish this relationship, it becomes easy to believe your standing as a princess and receive your inheritance. When this relationship is established masks fall off, wounds are healed, and walls come down. When this consistent intimate Jesus relationship is established, forgiveness of self and others occurs. Right boundaries are established in every area of our lives as a result of this intimate Jesus relationship. It is out of this relationship that purpose is revealed.

My challenge to you is to make a commitment to do what it takes to live Originally RED® for the next

90 days. Live out of your most authentic self as you allow God's truth and love to peel away the layers of false self you have accepted as your truth over the years. You may feel you already do this. If so, that's great. There is always room for check-ins and improvement. This challenge is still for you. If you feel like you have been hindered from living Originally RED® and some issues have come up for you as you read this book, I encourage you to dive fully into this challenge and make a plan for when and how you're going to tackle each step.

Originally RED® Challenge

- Write a letter to your 18-year-old self-regarding identity and purpose. Take your time with it. Put some thought, effort and prayer into it and see how God leads you.

- Write a letter to your daughter, future daughter or girls that you mentor about what your hopes and dreams are for them. This doesn't mean you give it to them necessarily though you could if you feel led. The exercise is more the revelation that will come out as you write to them from your heart.

- Ask God what areas He wants to shed His healing light on in your life? Write them down. Pray over these areas. Ask God to lead you as you submit these areas to Him.

- Journal your process daily if possible. Some women tell me they have a hard time keeping a journal. I can't relate (lol). I've kept a journal consistently since I was 16. I do understand everyone may not be able to journal in the same manner that I do. However, part of my challenge is for you to come up with a journal plan or system that works for you. I have traditional journals but sometimes using laptops and smartphones work better for people. I went through a particularly difficult season a few years ago. During that time, it was tough for me to write in a journal. So, I typed my journal daily on my laptop even if it was just one or two sentences. The reason keeping a journal is important is it enables you to track your journey with God. God has used my journals to remind me of things, confirm things, and track how far I've come. Another thing keeping a journal does is it shows you areas that continually trip you up. Sometimes it's hard to see these traps when you're in the midst of living day to day but when you can look back at months or years of journal writing, it becomes clear. One last thing and possibly my favorite reason for journaling is it provides a safe place for emotional release. During certain seasons, if I'm not journaling regularly, I feel like I'll explode. Journaling releases that pressure and also keeps me from sharing too much on social media (our girls desperately need this lesson). I can't say enough about keeping journals. It's a valuable habit to start and maintain.

- Create a Vision Action Board. I've been doing this consistently for several years now. I am not exaggerating when I tell you my boards have literally kept me going at times. As you embark on a commitment to live Originally RED, it helps to have visual reminders in front of you. Visit this blog post by one of my mentors Linda Dominique Grosvenor-Holland for detailed instructions on how to create a vision action board.

  http://www.lindadominiquegrosvenor.com-/how-to-create-a-vision-action-board/

It goes a step further than traditional vision boards. We typically think of vision boards when starting a new year. However, I feel they are a great activity to do anytime you embark on a major journey.

- Take part in a deliverance prayer ministry. I found this to be a critical part of my journey. Deliverance ministry is simply praying through areas of your life where healing is needed. I did this with another woman who was experienced in ministering to people in this way. Remember that deliverance often happens in layers. Even before I had my RED Revelation, I had gone through counseling and deliverance ministry. I still experienced blocks and all those walls didn't immediately come down. My RED Revelation happened exactly ten years prior to me writing this book. During those ten years, I have been on a journey of learning, growing, letting go, and healing. I believe being part of a solid, knowledgeable, spirit-filled deliverance ministry could have shaved some of that time off.

- Get an accountability partner. This is not something I'd do right away unless you know that you know who yours should be. One thing I've learned on my Originally RED® journey is how important your connections are. You need to have great discernment when sharing what God is doing in your heart. It is important to have someone to walk with you and agree with you in prayer but it's even more important that you have the person who is assigned to you for the season you are in. Don't pick who you think it should be. Ask God. He will show you.

- Lastly, I challenge you to reach out to me through the contact page at OriginallyRED.com and share something regarding your Originally RED® journey. Officially join the movement so my team and I (YES, there is an actual Originally RED® team) can pray specifically for you. We would love to hear from you and agree with you in prayer on your journey to wholeness or on your journey to being more equipped to lead others to wholeness.

Steps like this can be overwhelming and challenging to some. If you feel you need support and accountability on this journey, go to my website and look at the different coaching options that are available. I am available to support you.

Our families, friends, generations of girls behind us, communities and the world are waiting for us to be free enough, whole enough, surrendered enough to be Originally RED®; the women God originally destined for us to be. The world needs your RED mark!

Resources I have used on my healing journey of becoming Originally RED®:

Books and Ministries

- Experiencing The Father's Embrace-Jack Frost
- Keep Your Love On- Danny Silk
- Big Magic- Elizabeth Gilbert
- Born to Create- Theresa Dedmon
- Victory Over the Darkness- Neil T Anderson
- Bondage Breaker- Neil T Anderson
- Oh Lord, Forgive Them- Zari Banks
- Love Better Institute http://www.lovebetterinstitute.com
- Z TV - http://www.zaribanks.co/
- Worship Music from Eddie James (Yearn), Kim Walker-Smith and Jesus Culture(YouTube Channels)

Key Scriptures and Affirmations

On my Originally RED® journey, I have literally needed to post scriptures and affirmations everywhere to remind me who I am, who God is and the power I have in Him. They are in my car, bedroom and bathroom. I encourage you to do the same and say them out loud as often as it takes for you to get them deep down in your spirit. For me, that's daily and often. Also, I say them in front of a mirror at least one time per day. I find something extremely powerful about looking yourself in the eye and speaking these truths. I created a scripture sheet and an affirmation sheet for you to use on your journey. However, don't be limited by lists. God will illuminate certain scriptures to you for right where you are in your life.

Originally RED® Scriptures

These affirmations are based on scriptures. So as you speak them, you are covering your life with the Word.

- Submit to God. Resist the devil and he will flee from you. My hands are washed clean and my heart purified, my mind is made up and solely on Jesus. James 4:7

- I have been given power to tread on serpents and scorpions and over ALL the power of the enemy. Nothing shall by any means hurt me!!! Luke 10:19

- He who the Son sets FREE is FREE indeed. John 8:36

- Christ rescued me from the curse pronounced by the law. When He was hung on the cross, He took upon himself the curse for my wrongdoing. Galatians 3:13

- Therefore, there is now no condemnation for those who are in Christ Jesus. Romans 8:1

- God, who is rich in mercy and has great love for me, made me alive with Christ even when I was dead in my sins- I was saved by grace. Ephesians 2:4-5

- I am chosen, a royal priesthood, a holy nation, God's special possession. I will declare the praises of God who called me out of darkness into his wonderful light. 1 Peter 2:9

- I am thankful to God, who gives me the victory through our Lord Jesus Christ. 1 Corinthians 15:57

- The favor of the Lord God is resting on me; you have established the work of my hands – yes, you have established the work of my hands. Psalm 90:17

- Because I look to him, I am radiant, and my face shall never be ashamed. Psalm 34:5

- I praise you, for I am fearfully and wonderfully made. Wonderful are your works; my soul knows it very well. Psalm 139:14

Originally RED® Affirmations

Repeat affirmations out loud daily at least 3x/day. First thing in the morning and before bed are important times. Then pick your third time. Make one of those times while looking in the mirror.

- I Belong to GOD.
- I AM Accepted.
- I AM Loved.
- I AM FREE.
- I AM Secure.
- I AM Forgiven.
- I AM Significant.
- I AM Worthy.
- I AM Victorious.
- I AM Enough.
- I AM Whole.
- I have value.
- I believe God.
- ALL of my needs are met.
- I have the mind of Christ.
- The love of God is operating in my life.
- I AM perfectly loved by a perfect God.

I pray God's richest blessings over your life as you pursue healing and wholeness. I bind the forces of darkness that would try to keep you from walking out your days as healed, whole, submitted vessels operating under the power of the Holy Spirit. I release the love of God to flow in and through your life. I pray the soothing aloe of God's presence permeates every crevice of your heart and brings restoration to every wounded place. I am thankful for the resurrection of dead dreams and visions as you allow God to do His transformative work in you. I am praising God for the army of Originally RED® women arising to the call of God to get into position. You can only get in position as you acknowledge, understand, and believe your identity in Him. I pray that as you come into this understanding, a fire will burn inside of you to let your RED mark shine and impact a world of hurting women and children who have lost their Originally RED® selves.

In Jesus's Name,
Amen

Ladies, thank you for coming on this journey with me. It takes courage to be the woman God originally intended for you to be. It means you have to be open, honest, and focused on HIM. You have to be resilient. People and situations will try to knock you off course, but you have to let go of all that is holding you down continually to maintain your true identity in Christ. Be Bold. Be Brave. Be YOU!!! Be Originally RED®.

Stay connected at OriginallyRED.com and be on the lookout for:
- OriginallyRED®Unveiled Warriors (Book 2)
- OriginallyRED® Retreats
- OriginallyRED® Teen & Children's Products
- Join the OriginallyRED® FB Community for daily encouragement and motivation surrounding identity and purpose

ABOUT THE AUTHOR

Nicole Pertillar is an experienced counselor and certified life coach, a purpose pusher to women who feel stuck and unable to push past mess, hurt, disappointment, disillusionment and anything else that hinders them from walking in the call and purpose God has on their lives. Nicole is passionate about ministering to the hearts of women and girls. She has a strong voice of encouragement on social media speaking to identity and purpose. Nicole is currently developing the next book in the Originally RED® series. There is also an Originally RED® Facebook support group. Nicole resides in Harrisburg, PA and worships with the Harrisburg Justice House of Prayer (JHOP).

If you have enjoyed this book, please leave a review
online at your favorite retailer.

Additional copies of this book may be ordered at
your favorite online retailer and at
www.originallyred.com

R RAIN
PUBLISHING

www.ingramcontent.com/pod-product-compliance
Lightning Source LLC
Chambersburg PA
CBHW071623040426
42452CB00009B/1458